A Potpourri OF Garden Treasures

ART & TEXT BY MICHAL SPARKS

BLUE COTTAGE GIFTS™
a Division of Multnomah Publishers, Inc.
Sisters, Oregon

A Potpourri of Garden Treasures, a title in the Green Thumb Collection™

Text © 2001 by Michal Sparks
Published by Blue Cottage Gifts™, a division of Multnomah Publishers, Inc.®
P.O. Box 1720, Sisters, OR 97759

ISBN: 1-58860-002-5

Artwork by Michal Sparks
All works of art reproduced in this book are copyrighted by Michal Sparks
and may not be reproduced without the artist's permission. For more information
regarding art featured in this book, please contact:

    Mr. Gifford B. Bowne II
    Indigo Gate, Inc.
    1 Pegasus Drive
    Colts Neck, NJ 07722
    (732) 577-9333

Designed by Koechel Peterson & Associates, Minneapolis, Minnesota

Multnomah Publishers, Inc. has made every effort to trace the ownership of all poems and quotes.
In the event of a question arising from the use of a poem or quote, we regret any error made and
will be pleased to make the necessary correction in future editions of this book.
Scripture quotations are taken from The Living Bible (TLB)© 1971. Used by permission of
Tyndale House Publishers, Inc. All rights reserved; and from the Revised Standard Version Bible (RSV)©
1946, 1952 by the Division of Christian Education of the National Council of the Churches of Christ
in the United States of America.

Printed in China

01 02 03 04 05 06—10 9 8 7 6 5 4 3 2 1 0

www.gift-talk.com

Contents

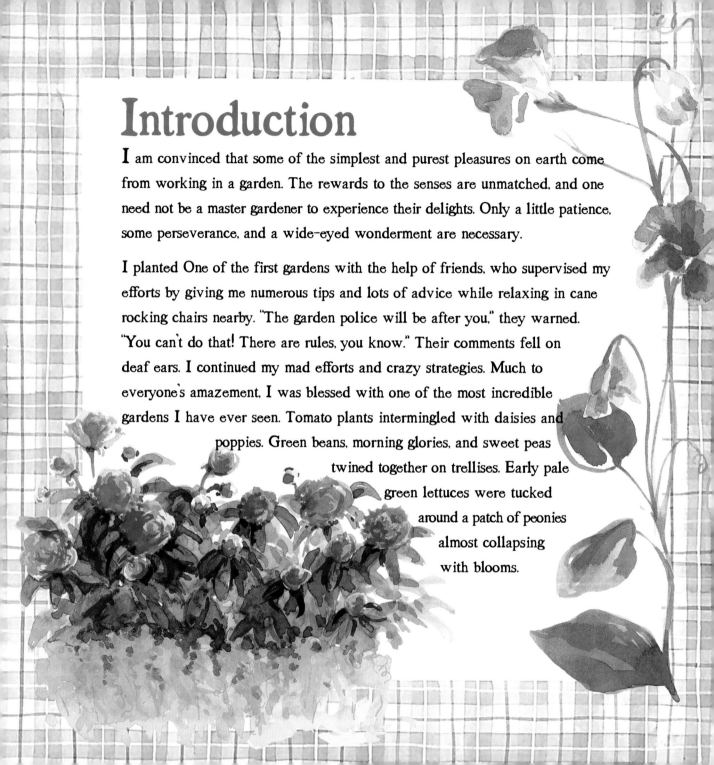

Introduction

I am convinced that some of the simplest and purest pleasures on earth come from working in a garden. The rewards to the senses are unmatched, and one need not be a master gardener to experience their delights. Only a little patience, some perseverance, and a wide-eyed wonderment are necessary.

I planted One of the first gardens with the help of friends, who supervised my efforts by giving me numerous tips and lots of advice while relaxing in cane rocking chairs nearby. "The garden police will be after you," they warned. "You can't do that! There are rules, you know." Their comments fell on deaf ears. I continued my mad efforts and crazy strategies. Much to everyone's amazement, I was blessed with one of the most incredible gardens I have ever seen. Tomato plants intermingled with daisies and poppies. Green beans, morning glories, and sweet peas twined together on trellises. Early pale green lettuces were tucked around a patch of peonies almost collapsing with blooms.

I continued gardening in this way for some years, until my husband and I purchased an old farmhouse located on ten acres. Now I had to learn to plan large, buy in bulk, and increase my stock of perennials by propagating my own plants.

I am not a master gardener, but I am a passionate one, and I hope some of my enthusiasm will find its way to you through the art, stories, and garden ideas found in this book. Have fun and break the rules! Try the unexpected and be amazed, as I was, at the potpourri of treasures a garden yields—the mix of delicacy and strength, the harvest of forgiveness and second chances, and the indescribable gifts that are given year after year.

Have fun and remember it's o.k to break the rules!

Michal

I am still devoted to the garden. But though an old man, I am but a young gardener.
 -Thomas Jefferson

Afternoon Tea: An Outdoor Cafe

Reinvent the afternoon tea party. Make this one a garden picnic—more relaxed, yet sophisticated, with soft, sun-washed cotton dresses and straw hats. Read aloud cherished time-honored classics, sip tea, and dine on small treats, iced and garnished with this garden's delights. An oversized bouquet of flowers cut fresh from the color-saturated border adds the finishing touch to a perfect afternoon.

Baby's Breath

Delphinium

Daylily

Daisy

I remember, I remember
The roses, red and white,
The violets, and lily-cups
Those flowers made of light!
-Thomas Hood

Purple Coneflower

Chamomile

Hollyhock

Violets

Outdoor Cafe

Hollyhock (Alcea)

Delphinium

Purple Coneflower (Echinacea)

Daylily

Shasta Daisy (Chrysanthemum)

Chamomile (Matricaria Chamomilla)

Baby's Breath (Gypsophila)

Linaria

Alyssum

Leaf Lettuce

Violets (Viola)

All of the flowers selected for this garden require full sun and are quite forgiving as far as soil goes.

Hollyhocks are best when backed up to a wall, building, or fence.

Don't be uniform when planting daisies and coneflowers. Try intermingling plants to give different colors and heights a chance to play off one another.

Cut down daisies for a second blooming later in the season.

Scatter baby's breath in front of daisies and other flowers. It will diminish the unsightly look of their foliage as the season progresses.

Leaf lettuce makes a pretty green border and is perfect for an afternoon salad!

As it fell upon a day
In the merry month of May,
Sitting in a pleasant shade
Which a grove of Myrtles made,
Beasts did leap and birds did sing,
Trees did grow and plants did spring.

-Richard Barnefield

A simple picnic cloth made from canvas provides hours of enjoyable spring and summer afternoons, especially for children. Who could resist a picnic?

Daylily

Chamomile

Violets

Daisy

Cone Flower

Chamomile

For centuries Chamomile has been used in tea to help soothe nausea and promote relaxation.

Harvest chamomile when flower heads are in full bloom.

Dry on a cloth or drying screen; remove any stems or leaves and store in an airtight container.

To make tea, use 2 tablespoons of dried flower heads in a tea strainer per 8 ounces of boiling water.

Edible Delights

For a very beautiful luncheon treat serve daylily petals! They have a subtle, sweet flavor and a slight crunch. Add a dollop of soft cream cheese or herbed sour cream. It's delicious.

Top off cheese and crackers with a sweet violet.

Pansies or Johnny-jump-ups, both completely edible, are magical when gently coated with egg whites then sprinkled or dipped in fine granulated sugar. It makes a sparkling treat.

Beautiful Refreshers

For a creative summer garnish, blanch mint leaves in boiling water, then freeze in ice cube trays for attractive ice cubes for tea.

Fresh scented and cool tasting, peppermint and spearmint make refreshing garnishes for summer drinks and soothing teas.

Garden Helpers

Ladybugs are probably the best-known biological pest control. The larvae and adults both eat small insects; aphids are their favorite.

Green lacewing larvae have an incredible appetite for aphids, mealy bugs, mites, whiteflies, and many other insect pests.

Praying mantises clean your garden of flies, mosquitoes, and moths.

The trichogramma wasp is a small but strong pest controller. It kills pests by feeding on their eggs before any plant damage can occur. The adult wasps are harmless to humans and animals.

Songbirds are rarely given credit for all they do. Many enjoy a snack of our most formidable pests.

Bats are your mosquito and gnat answer, if you can get past their colorful, if not scary, history. Bats consume at least 1,000 mosquitoes per night!

Sun & Spice: A Salsa Garden

Growing up in Texas, I naturally acquired a love for Mexican food flavors. So I always include a variety of peppers, tomatoes, and cilantro in the family garden. However, to really capture the essence of Mexico—the brightness of the hot sun and spicy flavors—I also enjoy adding some snappy flowers, bright and vibrant, cut for the table. It is a great way bring Tex-Mex to the East Coast.

Habanero

Cilantro

Jalapeño

Cayenne

Tomatillo

Beefsteak Tomato

Cherry Tomatoes

Salsa Garden

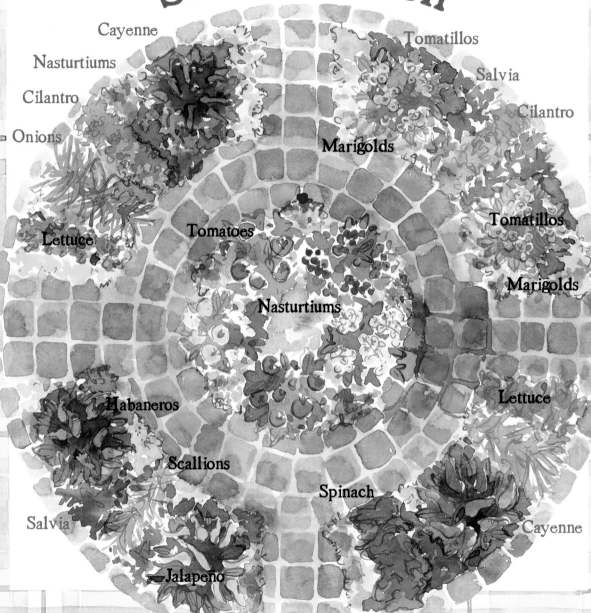

Cayenne

Nasturtiums

Cilantro

Onions

Lettuce

Tomatoes

Habaneros

Scallions

Salvia

Jalapeño

Tomatillos

Salvia

Cilantro

Marigolds

Tomatillos

Marigolds

Nasturtiums

Lettuce

Spinach

Cayenne

Tomatoes need six to eight hours of full sun. The best soil is well drained,

Tomatillos grow under the same conditions as tomatoes. They are indispensable for Mexican sauces.

Peppers, like tomatoes, need six to eight hours of full sun, even temperatures, and uniform watering.

Hot spicy peppers should dry as long as possible on the vine before harvesting.

Cilantro, commonly used as a Mexican food spice, is quite easy to grow in full sun and well-drained soil. Use the leaves fresh and let the plants go to seed. Gathered seeds are coriander! Two spices in one!

Lettuce grows quickly in cooler temperatures. Sow every two weeks until hot summer arrives, then again as cooler fall weather begins.

Beautiful Additions

Add south-of-the-border, sunny flowers to your garden, and cut them for your table. Sunflowers, Zinnias, Marigolds, and Nasturtiums are some favorites.

Zinnia

Sunflower

Nasturtiums in snappy red, yellow, and orange bring vibrance and fun to your garden, table, and plate. The flowers are edible, with a sweet but peppery flavor.

Marigolds not only add color to your garden but also repel certain insect pests.

Nasturtium

Marigold

Salvia

18

Chicken Breast with Salsa

3 chicken cutlets
2 tablespoons canola oil
2 tablespoons salted butter
8 ounces salsa
1/8 cup cilantro
4 tablespoons nonalcoholic
  margarita mix
1 cup flour

Pound cutlets to 1/2 inch thickness; coat with flour. In a frying pan, melt butter, add oil, and heat for one minute. Add cutlets, then pour on half the salsa, margarita mix, and cilantro, and cook on one side. Turn chicken and repeat. Make sure chicken is completely cooked, with no pink inside.

Serve with salad or Avocado with Santa Fe Mayo.

Garden Salsa

6 chili peppers (medium to spicy)
1 clove garlic
9 tomatillos, with husks removed
1/2 small onion, chopped
1/3 cup of chopped cilantro

Cook tomatillos in lightly salted boiling water for 5 minutes. Drain. Lightly brown chili peppers in a saucepan—no oil or butter is needed. In a food processor, blend tomatillos, chilies and garlic. Keep all juices. Transfer to serving dish and add remaining ingredients. This recipe makes about 1 cup.

Avocado with Santa Fe Mayo Topping

2 tablespoons mayonnaise
1/4 tablespoon garlic powder
dash of finely chopped cilantro
1/2 teaspoon nonalcoholic
  margarita mix
dash crushed red pepper
1/2 teaspoon cumin

Mix all ingredients together and let sit for 30 minutes. Serve on avocado halves on a bed of lettuce.

Vegetable Basket: Everyone's Garden

Of all gardens, probably the oldest and most popular is the vegetable garden. Everyone I know, even if they don't particularly like gardening, has at least a vegetable garden. I love to find unusual varieties of tomatoes and squash, and I can't seem to resist planting them all. Most of the time I end up overplanting, but I do try to leave a small space for the abandoned seedlings that mysteriously find their way to my front porch—usually with an anonymous note that reads, "I bought too many. I thought they would have a good home." Thanks!

Of all the wonderful things in the wonderful universe of God, nothing seems to me more surprising than the planting of a seed in the blank earth and the results thereof.

–Celia Thaxter

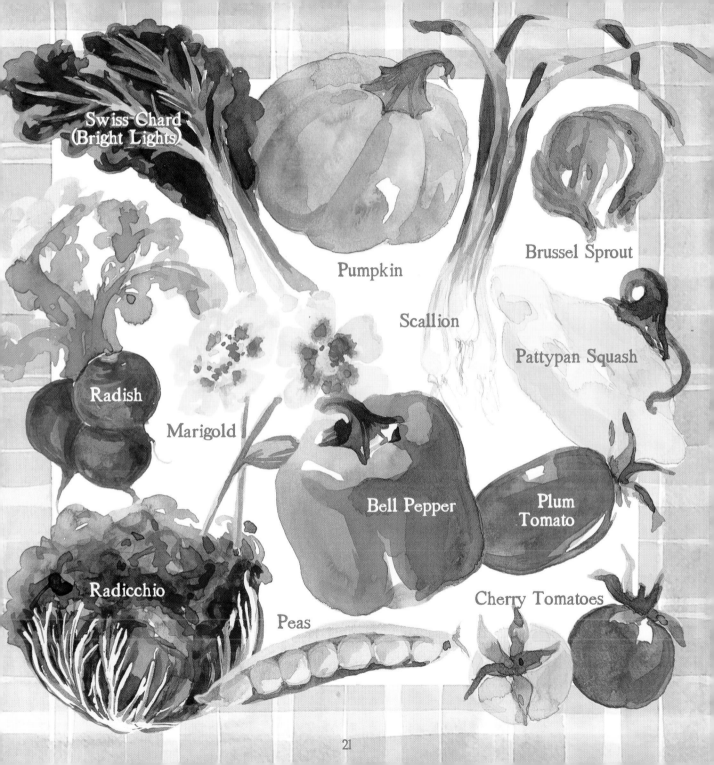

Swiss Chard
(Bright Lights)

Pumpkin

Brussel Sprout

Scallion

Pattypan Squash

Radish

Marigold

Bell Pepper

Plum
Tomato

Radicchio

Cherry Tomatoes

Peas

Vegetable Garden

Tomatoes

Tomatoes

Green Beans

Swiss Chard

Pepper

Eggplant

Lettuce

Lettuce

Oregano

Parsley

Happy
Gardener!

Basil

Rosemary

Herbs

Chives

Scallions

Cucumbers

Basil

Basil

Cilantro

Swiss Chard

Spinach

Radicchio

Pumpkins

Squash

Botanical Bits

A thick layer of organic material layered on your garden is always a good idea. Use compost, aged manure, grass clippings, seaweed, or shredded leaves.

Protect your garden from unwanted animal pests by planting chicken wire at least six inches deep around your garden and constructing a fence four to six feet high around it.

Planting vertically saves space and adds visual interest to your garden. Cucumbers, green beans, and peas are better off grown this way. They are less prone to disease when they are kept up off the ground.

When designing your vegetable garden, make a resting spot where you can sit and review your garden handiwork. It may also be the perfect place to relax and sample a fresh, sun-warmed tomato.

Place metal poles or rods next to tomato plants for support and added nutrition. It is thought that during thunderstorms they conduct nitrogen from the air and drive it into the soil.

Place half a grapefruit rind in your garden. Slugs and snails will climb in, and then you can easily discard them.

Radishes planted next to green beans will help ward off pesky insects.

To keep deer from nibbling away at your garden, hang pungent deodorant soap from nearby trees.

Make a mixture of very hot pepper and oil and spray on some plant leaves to discourage hungry rabbits.

Sampling sun-warmed vegetables right off the vine is just about the sweetest reward a gardener could ask for. Chemical free produce is a must, especially if your children tend to help themselves to a garden snack.

Basil Pesto

1 1/2 cups fresh basil leaves
2 cloves garlic
1/4 cup pine nuts
3/4 cup Parmesan cheese
3/4 cup extra virgin olive oil

In a food processor, blend basil, garlic, and pine nuts. Scrape the sides and add the oil and cheese; blend until it is the consistency of creamed butter. Serve over warm pasta with a side salad of fresh tomatoes sprinkled with balsamic vinegar.

Swiss Chard

1 pound fresh Swiss chard
2 cloves garlic, sliced
1/4 cup extra virgin olive oil
salt and pepper

Bring a pot of water to boil and add Swiss chard. When water boils again, remove the Swiss chard and drain it, then cut it up and place it in a large bowl with the oil, garlic, salt, and pepper. Let it sit for 10 minutes before serving to allow the flavors to mingle.

This is a wonderful side dish with chicken or fish. If you planted the "bright lights" variety, the colorful stems really jazz up your meal. It looks great and tastes delicious!

A Gardener's Portrait

Many years ago I read something similar to this passage while leafing through an antique garden book, and I must say, I agree! As old-fashioned and stuffy as this sounds, nothing beats a billowy linen shirt, softly worn khaki trousers or shorts, and a straw hat. And two items a gardener should never be without—I know I can't be— are rubber boots and leather gloves.

An honest gardener leaves vanity for another place and time, as nothing should overshadow the true reason for being in the garden. Clothing should always be kept to a level of comfort and utility. A pocketed apron used for tools should be the only embellishment, and minimal at that.

A Gardener's Motto

Something that I have noticed all over the country is that garden people all use the gardener's motto. It is universal, and every gardener has said it at least once, if not a dozen times.

At the end of a day of planting and weeding, when every muscle aches, ask gardeners anywhere how they feel, and they will say, "Whew, that was some job today. I got it done, but I'm tired." Then they will pause to think back over the day's work, and with eyes twinkling and the hint of a smile, they will say the universal motto of gardeners: "But it's a good tired."

Nature's Snacking Garden: Fruits & Berries

Some of my fondest memories of childhood include picking plums, pears, and peaches from my own backyard, and of course, risking life and limb to reach my neighbor's biggest, juiciest blackberries! I learned early that fruit trees and berry bushes make endless contributions to garden and table.

Spring Surprise

For many years gardeners have propagated fruit trees by grafting two or more types together. The purpose is to produce tastier fruit and stronger stock. Sometimes the result is a surprise. I have a very old sour cherry tree that had been grafted onto wild cherry stock. It was not pruned carefully, so in the spring it appears to be two trees in one: soft pink puffball blossoms below and a cloud of white flowers floating above. Now that is a surprise!

Espalier

Espalier training—one of the most beautiful ways to grow apple, pear, or peach trees—is efficient in many ways. Espaliered fruit trees save space when placed near a wall, preferably southeast or southwest, planted along a fence line or trellised. Because of the horizontal branch pattern, the fruit is more plentiful and easier to pick. This is especially true for pear trees. While fruit trees obviously enhance any garden, espaliered trees are centerpieces that delight the eye throughout the seasons.

Triple Horizontal   Wine Glass   Belgian Fence

Apples & Pears

Apples and pears thrive in similar conditions, and both should be planted in early spring in the North and late fall in the South.

Both, depending on their variety, need at least two pollinators within 100 feet of each other.

Fertilize once a year in early spring, and prune heavily in early spring or late fall.

When espalier training, branches must be pruned in early spring, then tied to a trellis through midsummer until branches harden into desired shapes. Prune in late summer and cut off all growth that is outside the pattern.

Cherries & Peaches

Cherries and peaches are usually better suited to warmer weather. If grown in cold climates, they should be well protected.

Plant and mulch peaches in the early spring.

Cherries should be planted in late fall in mild climates and in early spring in colder areas.

Sour cherries are self-pollinating, but sweet varieties require two specific pollinators.

With a few exceptions, peach trees are self-pollinating.

Use an all-purpose fertilizer once a year in the spring. Do not feed young peach or cherry trees until they are established.

Sweet cherries need to be pruned once a year in late winter to correct their overly vertical shape. Sour cherries need more center light, so prune once a year accordingly.

Raspberries & Strawberries

Raspberries and strawberries are very easy to grow and disease resistant. However, watch out for birds, deer, and hungry neighbors!

Both raspberries and strawberries should be planted in early spring and immediately after purchase to avoid shock. Apply compost to raspberries once each spring. Strawberries need well-composted soil from the start.

Both raspberries and strawberries are self-pollinating, but plant different kinds of each to enjoy the delicate differences of berry flavors.

Raspberries need pruning after bearing fruit. Red raspberries need to be thinned and the remaining canes topped at 48 to 60 inches. Black and purple raspberries need to be thinned and topped at 36 inches. Golden and everbearing red raspberries should be severely cut to 1 to 2 inches high, but only during the dormant stage.

Blueberries

Not only are blueberries delicious, but they also form a beautiful hedge with pink flowers in spring, produce healthy snacks in summer, and display vibrant foliage in autumn.

Plant two- to four-year-old plants in spring or fall. Apply an acidic mulch.

Blueberries need at least two pollinators, although a few self-pollinating varieties are now available.

Pruning is unnecessary except to cut off old or weak branches.

Basic Apple Pie

(Use this pie recipe as a guide and try different fruits and berries.)

7 or 8 apples, peeled and thinly sliced
3/4 cup granulated sugar
1/4 cup packed brown sugar
1/4 cup flour
1 teaspoon cinnamon and nutmeg
4 tablespoons lightly salted butter

Toss together all ingredients except butter and pour into uncooked pie shell. Cut butter into pats and dot the top of the apple mixture. Put on top crust and cut slits in top. Bake at 375 degrees for 25 minutes with foil covering edges. Remove foil and bake 25 minutes longer.

Perfect Pie Crust

2 cups flour
2 sticks lightly salted butter
   (cut into pats)
6 to 7 tablespoons cold water
1 teaspoon sugar

Awake, O north wind; and come, O south wind! Blow upon my garden, let its fragrance be wafted abroad. Let my beloved come to his garden, and eat its choicest fruits.
   –Song of Solomon 4:16, RSV

Combine flour, sugar, and butter pats in a food processor. Pulse until crumbly; slowly add water, then pulse. The dough should be crumbly but sticking together slightly. Divide and put into plastic wrap. While still wrapped, form into balls and chill at least 30 minutes. Roll out and place in pie pan, prick bottom with fork. Remember: Keep very cold and handle dough only the tiniest bit.

Victorian Love Notes: A Garden of Meanings

Peony
-bashfulness

Flowers have been providing us with romantic notions almost since the beginning of time, and we have responded by making them the center of stories and legends. My overactive imagination has always led me to create my own meanings and perceptions of flowers. The rose— she is the haughty queen of the garden. Daisies have the sincere smile of a good friend, and peonies, one of my favorites but sadly the garden's overachiever, work so hard to outdo all others with bloom and scent that they completely exhaust themselves and last but a short season. Next time you stroll down your garden's path, look again at your flowers and see if you wouldn't choose a different meaning than what history has handed down.

Yellow Rose
-friendship

Daisy
-innocence

Tussie-Mussie

Honeysuckle
-devoted
affections

Snapdragon
-presumption

A tussie-mussie, or poetic bouquet, reached the height of fashion in the Victorian era, when very discreet and knowledgeable young ladies and gentlemen corresponded with one another through a flower code known as the language of flowers. Certain meanings were given to all flowers, and it was hoped that everyone knew the same meanings. A flower or tiny bouquet of flowers would be sent to or from an admirer. A young gentlemen suitor might send a sprig of honeysuckle meaning, "I have devoted affections." Depending on her feelings, a young lady might respond by sending a pansy saying, "I, too, have tender thoughts," or maybe a snapdragon declaring, "You show much presumption."

Pansy
-tender thoughts

Victorian Garden

Red Rose

Phlox

Lavender

Anemone

Baby's Breath

Alyssum

Snapdragon

Daisy

Yellow Rose

Coreopsis

Thyme

Phlox

Lily-of-the-valley

Primrose

Astilbe

Forget-me-not

Hosta

Hosta

Hosta

A Wonderful Combination

This garden needs some sections that are in partial shade and sun and some that are in full sun all day. These flowers and plants like moist, rich, soil.

Hosta (Hosta) There are many colors and sizes available from four feet high to a dwarf size of eight inches. In late summer white or pale purple flowers appear on tall stalks.

Astilbe (Astilbe) Use these beauties on the edge of your shade garden. Blooms range from white to shades of pink and red.

Lily-of-the-valley (Convallaria majalis) Full shade is best. This one blooms early, so surround it with later blooming flowers.

Primrose (Primula) This flower is perfect for edging a shade garden and blooms from April through May.

Forget-me-not (Myosotis) In the shade, this plant will produce the most beautiful tiny blue flowers throughout the summer.

Alyssum (Lobularia maritima) Fragrant, tiny white flowers bloom all summer.

Hosta

Forget-me-not
-true love

Lily-of-the-valley
-return of happiness

39

No Shade, Please

These flowers and plants need full sun and rich, well-drained soil.

Thyme (Thymus) This plant is a hardy ground cover that blooms all summer. Plant on the edges of a path.

Baby's Breath (Gypsophila) Use to hide old foliage on daisies or coreopsis.

Coreopsis (Coreopsis) & **Shasta Daisy** (Chrysanthemum) Both these flowers will bloom again later in the season if you cut them back after first blooming.

Lavender (Lavandula) Blooms June through September.

Snapdragons (Amtirrhinum majus) Look for perennials as well as annuals. Blooms June through September.

Anemones (Ranunculacae) These plants need rich, moist soil and full sun. They have colorful blooms in August and September.

Roses (Floribundas) These can be pruned into a hedge that makes a spectacular backdrop. A grouping of two colors–red and yellow–work well in this garden.

Phlox These tall plants make a wonderful addition to any perennial garden.

Anemone
-desertion

Coreopsis
-forever cheerful

Bluebell
-delicacy

Zinnia
-simplicity

Freesia
-innocence

Columbine
-capriciousness

Bachelor Button
-hope in love

41

Anemone ~expectation

RedRose
~LOVE~

Lavender LUCK

Light is sweet, and it
pleases the eye to see the sun.

—Ecclesiastes 11:7, NIV

~Coreopsis~ Forever cheerful

Using small stones, copper, wood, or ceramic
markers, delicately write the meaning of each
flower in your garden next to its name.

Incorporate favorite flower meanings in the garden
path by painting tiles and carefully placing them
between the path and the brick edging.

Daisy ~Innocence

Thyme ~Thriftiness

But the roses they
were loveliest of all.
Never have I found in
the greenhouses of the North
such heart-satisfying roses as the
climbing roses of my southern home.
They used to hang in long festoons
from our porch, filling the whole air with
their fragrance, untainted by any earthy
smell; and in the early morning, washed
in the dew, they felt so soft, so pure, I could
not help wondering if they did not resemble
the asphodels of God's garden.

- Helen Keller -

Moonlight Reflections: A Nighttime Garden

With the world's technology filtering down into our everyday lives and with the constant access to one another, a place of peace and remembrance is desperately needed by us all—a quiet sanctuary to relax and reflect. When you enter the haven of a nighttime garden, time seems to stand still. Moonbeams dance on silver white petals, stars twinkle in the garden pond, and the subtle fragrances of rose, alyssum, and heliotrope mingle in the evening air. Close your eyes. Feel the peace.

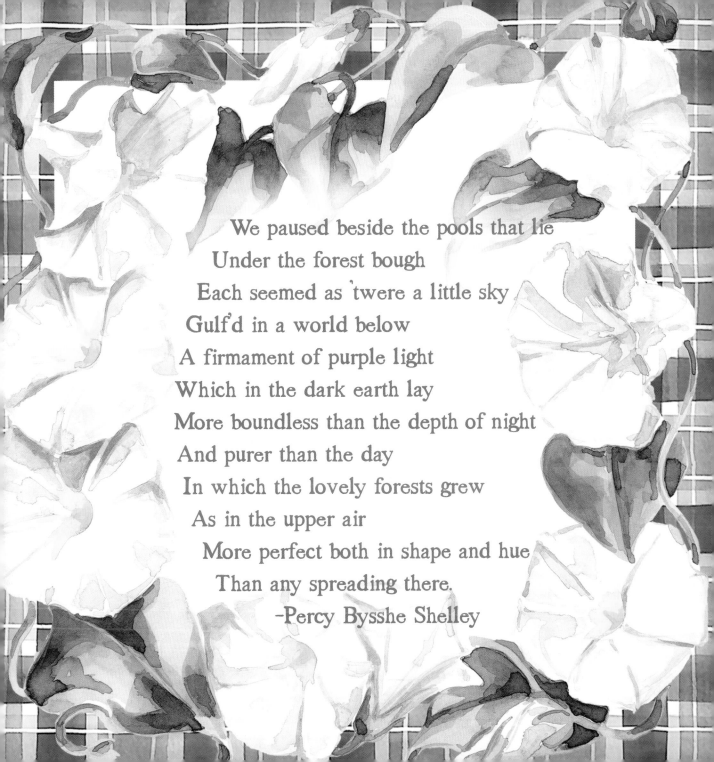

We paused beside the pools that lie
Under the forest bough
Each seemed as 'twere a little sky
Gulf'd in a world below
A firmament of purple light
Which in the dark earth lay
More boundless than the depth of night
And purer than the day
In which the lovely forests grew
As in the upper air
More perfect both in shape and hue
Than any spreading there.
-Percy Bysshe Shelley

Nighttime Garden

White Climbing Roses

Moonflowers

Heliotrope

Alyssum

Water Lily

Petunias

Dusty Miller

Lily-of-the-Nile

Heliotrope

White Climbing Roses These climbers cover
a trellis and arch to form the backdrop
of the garden.

Moonflowers (Ipomoea alba) These oversized
white flowers open in the evenings and close
up with the sunlight. The vines are beautiful
intertwined with roses.

Heliotrope Twenty inches high, it backs up to
the rose trellis. It blooms midsummer to fall.

Dusty Miller (Artemisia) Perfect for
reflecting moonlight.

Petunia They produce beautiful
flowers all summer.

Petunia

Dusty
Miller

A Perfect Addition

Think about adding a pond to your nighttime garden. Its reflective qualities will make moonbeams dance with delight.

Formal Design

approx. 30"

Natural Design

Bog

2 Feet

3 Feet

The design of the pond and the material it is made of is an important consideration in deciding what kind of plant should surround it. Any perennial or annual can border a cement pond with brick or stone edging. A pond with edges that are graduated calls for soggy soil and bog type plants for edging.

In warm evenings I frequently sat in the boat playing the flute, and saw perch, which I seem to have charmed, hovering around me, and the moon traveling over the ribbed bottom.

–Henry David Thoreau

Lily-of-the-Nile (Agapanthus)
This plant is perfect for an
oversized container.

Tuberose (Polianthes) A grouping of these fragrant
beauties will bloom late summer to fall.

Tuberose

Water Lily (Nymphaea ordorata) Plant is potted, then
submerged so that there is at least six to twelve inches of
water above pot. Almost all tropical lilies are fragrant. Some
open only at night.

Alyssum Planted randomly among the stones of the pond,
alyssum will subtly soften the edges and add a sweet fragrance.

Illuminating Ideas

Ivy or morning glories climbing
an arbor or on an obelisk or pyramid-
shaped form is a beautiful and easy way
to add height to any garden. Place a
few strings of outdoor twinkle lights
for a gentle nighttime glow.

To illuminate your garden, put a
little sand in a simple glass Ball
jar and add a tea light. The jar
will protect the flickering
candlelight from evening
breezes.

A stone birdbath close to the ground and surrounded by alyssum, ivy, or miniature hostas makes a simple, beautiful reflecting pool. Float tea lights for an extra glow.

God writes the gospel not in the Bible alone, but on trees and flowers, and clouds, and stars.

-Martin Luther

Fragrant Memories: An Aromatic Herb Garden

Breathe in the clean scent of lavender or the powerful perfume of jasmine, and thoughts of your grandmother's house will most likely come rushing in. She knew the secrets of scents, as did her grandmother. Thankfully, the wonderful

fragrances of herbs, plants, and flowers, which have enchanted the world for so many centuries, are easy to enjoy.

Scent that is nice for your nose is just part of their charm. Understanding and discovering how scents soothe, energize, or relax us is really an exciting part of gardening.

Rosemary

Lavender

Primrose

Violets

Rose petals

Simple Pleasures

Most of the herbs and scent flowers mentioned work well indoors if you plant them in well-drained soil, put them in a sunny window, and pay special attention to regular moisture and feedings.

Good drainage can be achieved by using a pot or a bowl with a hole in the bottom. Place it on a plate or tray. Or you can make a base of rocks, stones, or shards in the bottom of the pot before adding soil.

1

Soil

Rocks

2

Put pitcher in bowl
then add rocks or
pebbles & soil.

Primroses

3

Add plants
and water

Sweet Violets

Peppermint Lemon Balm

Violets

Chives

Oregano

Rosemary

Basil

Alyssum Thyme

Mixing bowl full of a mix of kitchen spices

Lemon
Balm

Lavender

Peppermint

Primrose in an
oversized cup
& saucer

Bucket full of energizing scents

A Banquet for the Senses

Pleasing is the fragrance of your perfumes;
—Song of Songs 1:3, NIV

Snip off a few leaves of peppermint and spearmint
and float in hot bathwater. This energizing soak also
soothes aches and pains.

A pot of lemon thyme provides a clean energizing scent
and is refreshing when dried in sachets.

Make a chamomile tea bath by filling a cheesecloth
pouch with dried flower heads and holding
under hot water while filling bathtub.

Float rose petals or sweet violet flowers
in bowls of hot water for a relaxing
steam for your senses.

Group together lavender,
alyssum, or wild thyme in
sachets to promote
relaxation and calmness in
your bedroom.

Lavender
Sachet

Chamomile
tea bath

Rose petal
& Violet steam

Rubbing the leaves of scented geraniums in a pot placed by the front door is refreshing whether you are coming or going.

Don't limit rosemary to the kitchen. Pots of it around the house are refreshing, and the scent is energizing.

Sachets of dried rosemary repel insects in closets.

An herb garden doesn't need to be a plot of land. A basket, crate, or tray of teacups filled with your favorite spices is a garden all in itself.

Thyme, parsley, chives and basil work well together in one container.

The more I study nature, the more I am amazed at the Creator.
-Louis Pasteur

Scented Geraniums

Nutmeg

Rose

Strawberry

Peppermint

Lemon

Rosemary

Rosemary closet sachet

Crystal Sculptures:
A Winter Garden

This is the season to reflect on the efforts of the year just past. Take a quiet walk on a brisk day and contemplate the trees, their branches crystallized as if by magic. The forms that leaves disguised in a warmer season now are bare garden sculptures. Stripped of color like a black-and-white photograph, their shapes and forms reveal inner beauty, meaning, and truth.

That time of the year thou may'st in me behold
When yellow leaves, or none, or few, do hang
Upon those boughs which shake against the cold
Bare ruin'd choirs, where late the sweet birds sang.
                    –William Shakespeare

The winter Garden lies at rest,
The clay upon her brows and breast;
The winding sheet drawn to her chin:
Her eyes blue the lids within.
Sleeping she hath within her arms
The wild songs and the soft charms;
The butterfly by her is laid,
The bee streaked in her chilly bed.
Alone-without leaf or bud.
What wild dreams stir her blood?
Under her hood what dream of mirth,
Of a new heaven and a new earth?
    -Katharine Tynan

Winter Garden

Holly

Holly

Holly

Colorado Spruce

Topiary

Weeping
Cherry

Kale

American
Arborvitae

Privet

Heath

Topiary

Kale

Weeping Cherry (Prunus Pendula) A fountain of pink flowers in the spring; beautiful branch shapes in the winter.

Holly (Ilex) Classic red holiday berries.

Colorado Spruce (P. pungens) A garden sculpture all in itself, the stunning blue spruce grows to at least seventy feet high and has a twenty-foot spread.

Privet (Ligustrum) This quick growing hedge loses leaves in cold winter weather, but the dense skeletal hedge is striking.

American Arborvitae (Thuja occidentalis) Although cone-shaped, its dense evergreen fan-shaped foliage forms a hedge.

Heath (Erica) Planted in groups, this hearty plant gives the effect of rolling hills.

Ornamental Kale (Brassiea deracea acephala) This dramatic plant with its low-to-the-ground height and circular shape adds the perfect touch of color.

Topiary A shaped shrub or ivy trained to a form, it adds fantastic dimension and depth to any garden.

Just Wing It

Make winter life a little easier for songbird friends. They help us with garden pests, so return the favor.

All day long the birds are singing
Sweetest songs that seem to rise
From their tiny throats far-reaching,
Even to the distant skies.
Then at night they rest securely,
Nestled close within their nest,
And the Father safely watches
Every little feathered breast.
Likewise we when night approaches,
Lay our weary heads to rest,
For we know that God will watch us
As He does the bird's wee nest.
　　—Josephine Currier

Birdseed, hulled sunflower seeds, suet, and peanuts are some food favorites.

Shrubs and bushes form a protective windbreak for little birds.

Small, cozy birdhouses are helpful for many birds and are great garden accents.

Certain shrubs and trees in your garden can help little birds through the winter, providing both berries and shelter. A large yew in my yard is home to many sparrows all year round.

All Around the House

Amaryllis (Hippeastrum) This winter favorite brightens up even the very darkest of winter days. Some say they can bloom for up to forty-five or fifty years.

Paper Whites (Narcissus) These flowers possess an incredible fragrance. Plant bulbs in pots every two or three weeks after September to have blooms to give away for the holidays.

Cyclamen (Cyclamen) This is a beautiful cold weather flower.

Paper White

Amaryllis

Cyclamen

Whenever I hear color forecasters talk about "earth-tones—the clean colors of nature," I laugh. Have these people been wearing blinders? They describe dull beiges, browns, and at best, terracotta. They seem to think that the earth is always the color of the dreariest of cloudy winter days. What about a vibrant summer blue sky mixed with the greenest greens of a field of corn? Haven't they noticed the red of a rose, the vermilion of a maple tree, or the scarlet of a sunset? These are the earth's tones! Nature follows no man's rules and her colors cannot be confined to manmade categories. As a gardener—a true nature artist—I am thankful and honored to be allowed to dabble, however clumsily, in the paint box of heaven.

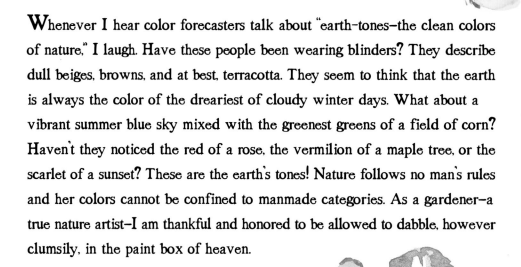

Spring is God thinking in gold, laughing in blue, and speaking in green.
-Frank Johnson